CHAPTER 1: WHAT I

Tea is the national drink of China and the practice of drinking tea has a long history in China.

According to popular legend the God of Medicine Shennong discovered tea by accident. Whilst boiling water under a tree, some leaves fell into the boiling water and he eventually drank the mixture. He found that the drink cured him of all ailments and from then on Chinese tea has been deeply woven into the history and culture of China and is believed to have medicinal properties that can prevent cancer and cure other diseases.

At its simplest, Chinese tea is a beverage made from the leaves of the *Camellia sinensis* and hot water but Chinese tea is more complex than that. In fact Chinese tea can be classified into five distinctive categories: white, green, oolong, black and post-fermented.

Yet more complex categories can include scented and compressed teas but all of these come from varieties of the *Camellia sinensis* plant.

Within these main categories of tea are vast varieties of individual beverages. Some researchers have counted more than 700 of these beverages. Others put the number at more than 1,000. Some of the variations are due to different strains of the Camellia plant and how tea leaves are prepared throughout the world.

The Tea Plant – Camellia Sinensis

Camellia sinensis is a species small tree whose leaves and leaf buds are used to produce tea.

Camellia sinensis is used for Chinese teas and *Camellia sinensis assamica* is used for Indian Assam teas.

The tea leaves are then transformed into the different categories of tea by a process of fermentation and oxidisation.

The *Camellia sinensis* grows to about 3 meters high and is native to southeast China. It is reported to have been first discovered, cultivated and used for tea over 3000 years ago.

Tea has always been believed to have medicinal properties and in most recent times in the Western world, tea has enjoyed perceived health benefits of weight loss, lowering cholesterol and being high in antioxidant which helps fight cancer.

Why Do We Call It Tea?

Tea is often called 'tea' or 'cha' depending on where you are. But why do we call it tea? If you've done a little travelling or have friends from different parts of the world, you'll notice that the word for tea in their languages is quite consistent with the English word ' tea'. For instances, the word 'tea' exists as is in Dutch, English, German, French, Italian, Spanish, Danish, Swedish, Norwegian, Finnish, Czech, Hungarian. This is based on the Latin pronunciation of 'te' a particular local dialect in coastal China. In fact, we can trace the origins of the word 'tea' to two main origins: the Minnan dialect and the Canton dialect.

The divergence, that is, where some countries use 'tea' and other countries use 'cha' is due to the historical trade routes that opened up China in the late 19th Century.

'Tea' comes from the Minnan dialect of Fujian province where it is pronounced 'te' and this area of China has had a long history of shipping and export.

The Chinese word for tea 'cha' comes from the Cantonese dialect and interestingly is the root of the words for 'tea' in Japanese, Russian, Indian, Iraqi, Turkish, Arabian and Portuguese.

Where And How It Is Grown

Tea only grows in warm climates and is mostly found in the band of regions between 16 degrees south latitude and 20 degrees north latitude. There are at least 34 countries that produce tea and the most important ones are located in Asia and Africa.

The basic process involves:

- cultivating the land
- sowing tea seedlings
- irrigating the land
- plucking the leaves
- processing the leaves

Cultivation of the land, sowing seeds and irrigating the land

Tea farmers weed and turn the soil so the roots of tea seedlings can penetrate deep into the earth to draw moisture and nutrients. Then the plantation is arranged into plots where seeds are sown. Three to five seeds are sown in evenly distributed ditches, and then covered with soil. After sowing, tea farmers have to water the seeds every morning and evening before they take root. After germination, irrigation is reduced to one every other day or even several days, just to keep the soil moist.

Plucking the leaves and tea yields

Tea yields vary from region to region and new leaves are ready for plucking from the 3rd year onwards. The best yields of the tea plant are considered to be in the 5th to 7th year.

Plucking is done at dawn before the morning dew is dry. Using the thumb and index finger, leave leaves are gently plucked by pressing down on them.

Depending on the variety, the pluckers will pluck one bud and one leaf, one bud and two leaves, or one bud and five leaves. The fresh buds and leaves must be transported to the factory for processing immediately; otherwise tea quality will be compromised. To speed up the process, tea factories are usually set close to plantations.

Tea is a perennial deep-rooted crop which can live for several decades. Unlike other short-lived crops that require replanting, tea plants develop new buds after each plucking to provide new yield. At the end of every harvest season, the plucking areas of the plants are pruned to keep them neat and maintain the height at a controlled level. After repeated plucking and pruning, the size of new leaves will be reduced and quality deteriorates. The plant is then chopped off from the roots up, so new branches can develop from the base. When they emerge, the tea plant is as good as new and ready for another long cultivation cycle.

Tea Growing Conditions

The conditions that tea plants grow in are extremely important not only for yield but also for the quality of the resultant tea leaves.

Climate

The tea plan prefers warm climates with a temperature range of around 10 degrees to 30 degrees Celsius. The reason why the tea plan does not grow outside of the latitude bands of 16 degrees south and 20 degrees north is because it does not adapt well to extremely hot or cold places. In essence, the climate needs to be mild for tea plants to thrive.

In China, the largest tea plantations are situated along the Yangtze River where it enjoys the mild climate. As a result this is an area with high tea output and at superior qualities.

Tea plants also prefer humid locations and places with 1,000 to 1,250mm annual rainfall are ideal for growing tea.

Terrain

Put simply, the higher the elevation, the richer its taste, and the better its quality. Tea thrives best in foggy and drizzly seasons where the soil can be kept moist. Areas that are 300 to 2,130 metres above sea level are best as these areas are generally shrouded in mist to block off the strong harsh sunlight. In addition, the slope must not be too steep. Maximum gradient is 25 degrees.

Soil

Tea plants require deep and fertile soil and grow best in pH4.5 - 6.5 red-yellow soils.

> *"Tea is one of the seven key necessities for any Chinese - wood, rice, oil, salt, soy sauce and vinegar being the other six."*

Tea Production And Processing

There are different processing methods that produce different varieties of tea. Fermentation is one of the key factors differentiating different tea varieties.

Teas can be categorised into non-fermented, semi-fermented, full-fermented, and post-fermented tea.

The oxidation and fermentation process of the harvested tea leaves impacts the kind and quality of the tea produced. These 2 processes have an impact on the taste, colour, aroma, and nutrition values of the tea; and even the lifespan of the tea.

Although the level of oxidation and fermentation is different, all tea varieties go through several key production steps: picking, withering, pan firing, rolling, fermentation, roasting, and sieving.

General process

Impurities like yellow leaves, old leaves, and stalks have to be picked out from the harvest. After picking, tea leaves have to go through a withering and pan firing process. Withering means spreading out the plucked leaves to breathe. The aim is to remove moisture and promote enzyme activity to facilitate chemical changes within the leaves. This process is necessary for the production of oolong, white, and black tea, where oxidation is necessary to produce the chemical compounds that create their flavours and characteristics; and the presence of enzymes promotes and facilitates such oxidation.

Green and yellow teas go through a firing process right after they are harvested to prevent from oxidation. Fresh tea leaves are processed at high temperatures to stop the enzyme activity. As a result, tea leaves become soft, tender and easy to roll.

Once withered, leaves are rolled in order to stress and crush the cells causing friction so that the juice spills over the surface of the leaves and make them contract and twist. This is how tea leaves are moulded into long spirals.

The enzymes in the tea are oxidised once they are in contact with the air, this happens during the fermentation process. When the leaves begin to oxidise, the resulting chemical reactions turn the leaves from green to copper. This is when expert tea makers adjust the duration and the temperature (as well as the humidity) of the oxidation process to produce the taste, colour and richness of their teas.

Following the expert craftsmanship of the tea makers, the tea leaves are then roasted in high temperatures to quickly evaporate any residual moisture. During this time, enzyme activity is stopped to prevent tannin oxidation which gives the tea a bitter taste. This is all done to the desired colour, aroma and taste of the tea that the tea maker decides to produce.

Traditional roasting is done on a big pan on coal fire and some factories still use this method. The final step is sieving. The tea workers sieve out loose bits and spread the tea out to cool over bamboo sifters. The sifted tea leaves will then be ready for grading and packing and onwards for distribution.

Stages of tea production

Withering

The picked leaves are spread out both indoors and outside in the sun in order to soften the walls. This draws the moisture of the leaves to the surface for evaporation and prepares the leaves for fermentation. Softening the cell walls also encourages the natural enzymes to start working for the next stage. This process also reduces the grassy taste of the tea leaves.

Tossing/Bruising (Turning Over)

Tossing, bruising or turning over is also known as 'shaking' in Chinese as traditionally, the leaves were shaken in wicker baskets. In modern times, this process is carried out by machines that help further break down the leaves. This is in contrast to the chemical breaking down of the leaves of the first stage: withering. The mechanical breaking down of the leaves improves oxidation and encourages the mix of chemical elements from the stems and leaves and removes the bitterness of the tea. This process is about balancing the flavour of the tea.

Oxidization (Partial and Full)

Oolongs and black teas are allowed to rest after the withering and turning over steps to continue the natural process of fermentation. The duration of the fermentation determines the intensity of the flavours and the type of tea being made. The tea leaves turn a darker green or even red as the cell structure of the tea leaves continue to break down. The tea leaves start to develop its flowery, fruity or grassy characteristics.

"Kill-Green" or Fixing"

As the name suggests, this is the stage that stops the natural fermentation process in the leaves without damaging them. This is achieved by steaming them, hand pressing in a hot pan or backing techniques. By doing this, the tea leaves will then become most malleable for rolling or forming of the tea leaves as we know them.

Rolling or Forming

The leaves are then passed through hot and/or cold rollers to break down the leaves further, intensifying the flavours and creates the shape of the leaves.

Drying

Drying sops the fermentation and locks in the final moisture content of the tea. Drying also prevents mould growth and removes any remaining grassy taste whilst it develops the tea's aroma. Methods of drying include pan heating over hot coals, drying in the sun or using hot air.

Firing

This step is used for oolongs to give it the smoky flavour characteristic of this type of tea. It can also give the tea its fruity notes. Firing is achieved by roasting in a pan or a basket over charcoal or electric heat.

Piling/Heaping

Black Pu-Erh tea undergoes this additional step whereby the leaves are heaped into a pile to be moistened, covered and allowed to rest in a warm environment. This speeds up the natural fermentation process and the heat caused by the fermentation process "cooks" the leaves. This gives the tea its mellow taste and distinct dark colour.

Steaming/Shaping

Pu-Erh tea leaves are then steamed and moulded into their specific shapes before packing.

The Benefits Of Chinese Tea

There are many health benefits attributed to drinking Chinese tea, ranging from feelings of well-being to near magical cures. For the Western world, the focus and increased interest revolves around claims of weight loss and cancer prevention due to the antioxidant properties of tea. Whether this is true or not is still debatable. In short, there is little scientific consensus on the health properties of tea. Therefore everyone should make their own assessment of the health benefits of tea.

For the Eastern world, the focus is more on the art of drinking tea and enjoyment of tea for its flavours and aromas. While it is true that according to traditional medicine there are positive and negative energies in what we eat and drink, it's once again, not supported by science yet. It's not the intention of this book to suggest drinking tea to prevent or cure cancer or to achieve weight loss but merely that tea should be enjoyed for its intrinsic values and not necessarily its perceived health attributes.

That being said, there are certain properties of tea that are clearly identified to have health effects such as caffeine and how it is used in traditional Chinese medicine.

Caffeine

Tea has caffeine. Simple as that. It's often being recommended that coffee drinkers drink tea in order to lower their intake of caffeine and no sooner has someone suggested that that someone else decries "but tea has more caffeine than coffee!'. Which is correct and who do you believe? Both statements are correct to a degree and it's quite dependent on the type of tea, how the tea was made, how the tea is consumed and in what quantities.

Caffeine in tea and coffee compared:

    All Teas on average have 40 mg per serving

    Instant Coffee on average has 54 mg per serving

    Ground Coffee on average have 105 mg per serving

There's a popular belief that Chinese green tea has less caffeine than black tea. The discussion and studies around this topic suggests that it might be quite the opposite. It's not really known where the confusion arises, perhaps possibly due to the colour difference or the recent health trend that promotes the 'health properties' of green tea over all other sources. But what is clear is that these two types of teas cannot be compared in such a way because these two types of teas are completely different in its genesis, production and drinking custom. As we've discussed before, these are all very important factors in determining whether one has more caffeine than another.

Most black tea exported to the West is from India and the *Camellia assamica* plant from which Indian tea is made produces higher levels of caffeine than from the *Camellia sinensis* variety that is used for Chinese teas.

Further to that, the oxidisation process in the Chinese black tea production process reduces the caffeine content rather than increasing it – which was what, was previously thought. Therefore in comparison of Chinese black tea to Chinese green tea, caffeine of Chinese green tea would seem higher than in Chinese black tea. However both are considerably less than Indian black teas and all teas is significantly less than coffee.

Therefore caffeine levels are relative and depend on the types of tea you drink as well as how the tea is made.

How you prepare the tea for drinking also impacts the levels of caffeine in the resulting drink. For instances, a way to control the levels of caffeine of any tea is to use the traditional Chinese method of tea-making known as Gong Fu Cha or more commonly known as a Chinese tea ceremony. This method of drinking tea uses small tea pots, multiple brews and very short steeping times. This highly controlled method intensifies the flavour of tea and does not allow the caffeine levels to get high due to short steeping times. Most of the caffeine is also washed away in the first brew which is often used to wash the leaves rather than for drinking. As caffeine is highly soluble in water, the caffeine is not retained in the tea leaves for the second and subsequent brews that are for drinking.

Traditional Chinese Medicine

Listed below are commonly held beliefs in traditional Chinese medicine of the health properties or benefits of each type of tea. These beliefs are held in traditional Chinese medicine but not necessarily supported by science either due to the lack of scientific study in the area or the constant debate between the effectiveness of Eastern and Western medicine. These are listed for reference purposes rather than suggestions and recommendations on diet and nutrition.

Black Tea

- Reduce fat, protein and low-density "bad" cholesterol
- Rich in fluoride, promotes dental health
- Reduce fatigue, stimulating the central nervous system
- Promotes strong bones
- Enhance blood vessel elasticity and strength

Green Tea

- Have anti-bacterial and anti-virus properties
- Regulates cholesterol and high blood pressure
- Bacterial killing properties in the mouth and intestines
- Can lower blood sugar
- Improves blood flow

White Tea

- Can reduce inflammation caused by rheumatoid arthritis
- Can control insulin secretion
- High source of Vitamin A, can prevent dry eyes and night blindness
- Can reduce radiation levels and repair DNA damage

Oolong Tea

- Polyphenols prevent tooth decay
- High source of Vitamin C, good for the skin
- Can reduce skin irritations
- Can improve the performance of enzymes that break down fat and increases fat metabolism
- Can lower cholesterol

- Muscle relaxant in the bronchial tract
- Can regulate body temperature

Pu-Erh Tea

- Aids digestion and fat break down
- Has been used in the treatment of arteriosclerosis, colds, bleeding and hepatitis
- High level of Vitamin C which is soluble in water and can be rapidly assimilated by the body

CHAPTER 2: THE HISTORY OF CHINESE TEA

Tea is one of numerous inventions of the Chinese. It is said to have been discovered by the God of Medicine Shennong and like all legends, quite by accident.

Today, Chinese tea is used as tonic at Chinese tea houses, cafes and at home. It is also drunk at special ceremonies such as weddings and most often found as a staple in any restaurant or home.

There are many versions of how Shennong discovered tea and created the tradition of drinking tea.

The first version of the legend describes a Shennong with a clear and transparent belly so that everyone could see whatever he ate. He travelled the wilderness to try every herb in existence. He did so in order to protect the people from disease, ailments and poisons. It is said that one day he tasted some fresh leaves of a certain plant and found that they moved around in his belly. He deduced that they were 'inspecting' something and named them 'zha' (meaning check) and as time went on the leaves became known as 'cha'.

The second version of the legend, and perhaps, the most popular one is that Shennong went around tasting herbs and was poisoned by no less than 72 different plants every day. After a particular frightful tasting, he almost died under a tree. He was only saved by the fresh dew on the leaves that dropped into his mouth. That's when he discovered the medicinal value of tea.

The less poetic version of the legend has Shennong boiling water under a tree one day and the leaves fell into the pot. He mistakenly drank it and all his toxins and ailments disappeared.

No matter which version of the legend you choose to believe (or not believe), we have Shennong to thank for the discovery of the medicinal properties and purposes of tea.

Brief History Of Tea

As the legends of Shennong suggest, tea was used for medicinal purposes long before it was the national beverage of choice.

The tradition of drinking tea originates naturally in the regions of China where tea grows: western Sichuan and the southern region of the Yangzi River.

The custom of drinking tea gained popularity in the Han dynasty (206 B.C. - 220 A.D.) and the Southern and Northern Dynasties (386 - 589 A.D.). Tea drinking continued to spread across China, but it wasn't until 8th century, during the Tang dynasty, that tea drinking became a national custom.

Tea drinking customs developed with the times and with the advancement of society. For instances, tea was initially used for medicinal purposes and was considered quite bitter by any standards. Tea cultivation back then was not about enjoyment, but about medicine. Then tea drinking evolved and recipes and customs developed out of how people lived and the values of the time.

Tang Dynasty - 618 - 907 AD

Drinking tea was only popular with people of the southern regions of China until the Tang dynasty brought it to the whole of the country. Prior to this, people mainly prepared tea by boiling water and adding tea leaves to it along with spices.

Tea drinking gained momentum in the Tang dynasty because of the rise in popularity of Buddhism. A popular theory is that Buddhist monks spent long hours meditating and in a state of high focus but whilst their scriptures forbid them from consuming stimulants, it did not speak of consumption of tea. Tea, as you know, contains caffeine and the monks discovered this early on as a means to fight off drowsiness and to stay hyper-focused during these meditative sessions.

Soon after, everyone adopted the practice of drinking tea and made the tea drinking process a spiritual experience, even creating ceremonies for it. Slowly but steadily, tea drinking became an integral part of Buddhism and thus was the beginning of the spread of tea drinking as a custom.

In a few short decades, tea drinking became a national custom in China.

he Tang people had different methods of preparing tea as a beverage. History has shown that the Tang people boiled tea leaves in a pot together with ginger, leek, mint, date, dogwood, and orange peel, quite similar to what the people of the Han dynasty did.

Another popular method was to steep the tea in hot water after the tea had been chopped, roasted and pounded.

And finally, tea was also ground into powder form and was added to boiling water along with some salt. The tea drink was then served in a tea bowl.

Song Dynasty – 960 – 1279 AD

In the Song dynasty, tea drinking became a marker of the social and intellectual life. Offering tea to visitors became a universally accepted practice and many scholars, officials and nobles became experts in the preparation of tea. Tea parties became popular during this period and tea was produced in the form of scented tea cakes.

The Song dynasty can also be attributed with the invention of the 'whipped tea' method of tea preparation. This is where tea is first ground into a fine powder and a vast quantity was place into a tea bowl. After the hot was has been added to the tea bowl, the mixture is whipped with a bamboo whisk to froth it.

During this period, the tea preparation process was seen as a meditative process that soothes the mind and much attention was paid to the different steps of preparing the bowl of tea.

Yuan Dynasty – 1271-1368 AD

In the Yuan dynasty, tea drinking evolved yet again with the addition of cream. Before serving tea, cream was added to the bowl of tea and its practice is most likely due to the Mongolians who conquered China in the 13th century.

It was also around this time that team makers invented various ways to scent the tea with fragrant flowers.

In this period, people ate different kinds of nuts such as walnuts, pine seeds, sesame, almonds, and chestnuts together with their bowls of tea which gave rise to the habit of tea becoming part of the meal. This habit later developed into the modern day practice of serving tea with 'dim-sum'.

Ming Dynasty 1268-1644 AD

In the Ming dynasty, people preferred to prepare tea by steeping refined tea leaves in a teapot and thus the 'steeping method' was born.

The amount of tea leaves used and the water temperature were carefully controlled in order to create a good cup of tea.

At the beginning of the Ming dynasty, people used large teapots to brew tea so that many cups could be produced from one pot of tea. They later discovered that too long a steeping time of the tea leaves produced a tea that was bitter and the last few cups from the teapot were not as fresh as the first few. Consequently, tea pot sizes became smaller and smaller and teapots became prized possessions with teapots from the Yixing region, made of purple clay, particularly prized.

Qing Dynasty – 1644 – 1911 AD

Tea preparation by steeping continued into the Qing dynasty and more attention was placed on the quality of the teapots used. The purple clay teapots of Yixing quickly became the favourite as it was often said that they were the best ones in bringing out and retaining colour, flavour and aroma of tea.

Teapots of pewter and porcelain were also prized for being able to keep tea warm for longer periods of time.

It was also around this time that the people of the Qing dynasty used covered teacups to brew tea. Covered teacups are ideal for preparing tea for one person and not necessarily suitable for groups of people, however, it is not unheard of.

Qing dynasty tea makers were able to control tea fermentation by special methods which resulted in the production of black tea and oolong tea. It was finally in the Qing dynasty that people had the choice of selecting different types of tea.

With new teas came new methods of brewing teas such as the traditional method of brewing Chinese tea that we know today as gong fu tea or Chinese tea ceremony.

Popularity Of Tea In The Modern Age
Health benefits – fitness, weight loss

We've briefly touched on the perceived weight loss benefits of various types of Chinese tea. They include green teas and black teas for both their antioxidant properties as well as their fat burning properties. Whether they're effective still remains to be seen but indeed it is the custom to drink Pu Erh tea with meals and 'dim-sum' for their perceived benefits of 'balancing' and aiding in digestion.

Traditionally the drinkers of tea have been elderly people but with the new perceived health and fitness benefits of tea, there is an increasing market of young tea drinkers, particularly as they discover scented and flavoured teas.

Genmaicha and green teas

Although not strictly Chinese tea, Genmaicha has increased the profile of tea in general in Western media. Genmaicha is a Japanese green tea mixed with puffed brown rice and often tastes nutty and roasted, like popcorn.

Genmaicha is made with various kinds of green tea and research has linked drinking genmaicha regularly, to prevention of disease and overall health benefits. These benefits include:

- Antioxidants
- Cancer Prevention
- Low Blood Pressure
- Heart Health

As an investment for the burgeoning Chinese middle class

With the rise of China's middle class and purchasing power, tea went through a particularly turbulent resurgence in the early to mid-2000.

Suddenly flush with money, the burgeoning Chinese middle class searched for investment opportunities, first in property, then in wine and since the early 2000s: tea.

The popularity of tea as an investment, and particularly Pu-Erh tea, is due to a few variables:

- Market size
- Ability to be kept for long periods
- Health benefits

The market for Pu-erh tea is relatively small, with only about 20 million to 30 million consumers worldwide and the average compounding return of 10% a year makes it a very attractive investment opportunity.

Pu-Erh tea is popular for investing because, like wine, it gets better with time and it can be stored for long periods of time, reportedly for 100 years or more. Also similar to wine, the genesis of the tea can be analysed along with the 'terroir' and the whole tea production process.

The perceived health benefits of pu-erh tea continue to fuel the popularity and investment in them.

As with all investments in commodity goods by the Chinese, it becomes a clear sign of status and wealth.

However it is an investment that is not without its controversy.

There is no consistent valuation method or quality check that the wine industry enjoys and more often than not consumers are the ones that are being short-changed. The value of a particularly type of Pu-erh of a specific origin is quite open to interpretation and there are no independent critics or valuation system like in the wine industry.

The tea as an investment trend quickly became chaotic when prices for Pu-erh doubled and even tripled as people were buying anything and everything that remotely resembled Pu-erh tea. As a result in 2007, Pu-erh tea was –quite literally – worth its weight in gold. When this threshold was reached the market was suddenly flushed with fakes or poor quality teas and the prices plummeted. This was regarded as a big tea bubble finally bursting.

As a consequence, the Chines government intervened in order to restore confidence in Chinese teas as well as to assure tea investors. Beijing tightened controls that defined what a real Pu-erh should be similar to the denomination of origin of wines. From December 2008 onwards, only teas from the Yunnan province's 639 towns can be labelled Pu-erh.

Yunnan leaves aged outside of the province would no longer be considered authentic and certain branded teas must contain certain type of leaf.

However these standards and controls only apply to domestic producers in China and do not regulate the competitors in other tea producing countries such as Vietnam, Sri Lanka and Burma who continue to grow and sell their own Pu-erh teas.

Resurgence of religious overtures and ceremonies

Tea drinking has always been closely tied to the practice of religions, particularly Buddhism. Therefore it is no surprise that the popularity of tea increases in direct proportionality to the popularity of religions or practice of certain religions.

For instances, the practice of Japanese Zen and the art of the tea ceremony saw the increase in popularity of green teas.

Variations include Korean tea ceremony and of course the traditional Chinese tea ceremony or gong fu ceremony. These are practiced for their meditative benefits.

CHAPTER 3: HOW TO DRINK TEA

Tea Etiquette And Customs

Tea is a cure all for many ailments and increasingly is being used in place of hot boiling water to clean bowls and utensils at the table. This is particularly prevalent at restaurants where it's perceived that utensils and serving bowls are unclean. I had observed this behaviour first in Hong Kong during the SARS epidemic and everyone was becoming hyper aware of hygiene. Being a sharing culture, meals are taken together and multiple dishes are ordered at once to share with the entire table. This of course raises concerns regarding hygiene and as a precaution, this practice of washing the bowls and utensils beforehand emerged.

It's perceived that bowls and utensils will be sterilised by the tea and it is not uncommon to see in restaurants a large plastic bowl and tea pots full of lower grade oolong tea and for people to start pouring the tea over bowls and utensils into the large plastic bowl.

Customs of ethnic groups within China

China is a vast country with a long history. China is also home of 55 ethnic minorities representing 6.7% of the total population and covering 60% of the total area of China. Therefore there is no consistent pan-Chinese way of preparing or drinking tea.

With China's long 5000 years of history, different groups of different geographic locations, environments and cultural heritage have developed their own styles of tea drinking. These styles have developed over the course of time and have enriched the culture of tea drinking as a whole.

Each ethnic group has its own unique tea drinking custom, such as gongfu tea of Fujian, green tea of Jiangnan, covered tea bowl tea of Chengdu and Chongqing, morning tea of Guangzhou, nine-course tea of Kunming, "big bowl" tea of Beijing, Mongolian milk tea, etc.

Kazakh – Milk tea

Kazakh nomads have milk tea 3 times a day at morning, midday and in the evening. Elderly Kazakhs also take more milk tea in the morning and the afternoon.

Kazakh milk tea is served with roast mutton, baked wheat pancake, honey, cream and apples. Kazakh milk tea is considered a nutritious drink that is beneficial to digestion a therefore consumed by everyone.

Kazakh milk tea is made from boiling black tea leaves, cardamom and fennel seeds. Milk or cream is then added to the mix along with sugar or honey to sweeten it.

Tujia - Pounded Tea

Tujia pounded tea is also known as lei cha and is prevalent with the Hakka people.

Pounded tea is taken as a kind of food, or gruel, to fill up the stomach as well as to keep the body warm. Pounded tea consists of mixing tea leaves with herbs and pounded together with various roasted nuts, seeds, grains and flavourings. The tea is drunk for breakfast or on cold winters as a tasty and healthy restorative.

Lei cha taken as a food is served with rice and other vegetarian side dishes such as greens, tofu, and pickled radish.

Making savoury pounded tea is much like the process of making rice gruel or vegetable soup. The fresh tea leaves are pounded with raw ginger and raw rice and other spices and flavourings and boiled until it is a soup like consistency.

Miao - Eight-treasure oil tea

The Miao people are known for drinking oil tea and in particular one that is called eight-treasure oil tea. Different foods are added into the oil tea and are therefore considered more of a tea soup or food. The tea brew carries a delicate aroma due to the sophisticated tea-making process and the carefully chosen ingredients.

The oil tea is made by first deep-frying the corn that has been left to air dry, soybeans, peanuts, rice cakes, diced dried bean curd, and vermicelli separately with tea-seed oil, and then put them into different bowls for serving later.

The tea soup is then served to guests.

Naxi - Longhudou Tea

This is a drink that is part tea and part white spirit. In other words, longhudou tea is slightly alcoholic. A small amount of tea leaves is added into a small pottery pot and roasted over fire. The pot is kept turning and roasting so that the tea leaves can be heated evenly and not burn. When the tea leaves produce a burning aroma, boiling water is quickly poured into the pot and kept burning for another 3-5 minutes.

To serve, a tea cup is then filled with some kind of white spirit and filled to halfway. The boiling tea mixture is then poured into this spirit filled cup producing a crackling noise. The Naxi people believe the sound is auspicious and the louder the sound, the happier the people will be.

Blang - Bamboo tea

The Blang people enjoy bamboo tea. They live in an area that produces pu-erh tea leaves and tea cultivation is an important source of income for the Blang people.

Blang people prepare a tea called 'bamboo tea' which is drunk during farming or hunting outdoors.

Bamboo tea is prepared by taking a bamboo tube and cutting a big hole out of it, sharpened at one end and staked into the ground. It is then to be used to make tea. Water is poured into it and some dry twigs are placed around the tube to be burnt and creating heat. When the water in the bamboo tube boils, tea leaves are added and left to boil for up to 3 minutes. The tea is then ready to be served in pots made of bamboo stems.

Bai - Three course tea

Bai people have a dramatic tea ceremony that is often called a 3 course tea ceremony where each course lasts from 3-5 minutes.

The first course of tea is called "bitter tea" which implies the philosophy of life that "to start a career, one has to endure hardship first".

The second course of tea is called "sweet tea". After the guests finish the first course of tea, the host will again put tea leaves into the small clay pot, and then roast and boil the tea leaves. Meanwhile, the host has to add some brown sugar, cow's milk cheese and cassia into the teacup and then pour the tea into it until it is 80% full.

The third course of tea is called "aftertaste tea". While the method of making tea is the same, the ingredients are replaced with a moderate amount of honey, a little popped rice, several pieces of wild pepper, and a handful of walnut seeds. The teacup is usually filled to 60-70%.

Tea Selection

Tea selection is vital to tea drinking but there is no right or wrong way to select tea. It all comes down to taste. However with so many teas to choose from where do you start?

Here are 4 basic steps that can help you determine if the tea is a high quality tea or not.

1. Observe and inspect.

Higher quality teas or fresh tea have a green lustre and they're in a tight shape. Poor quality teas are loose and dull in colour. Take a few leaves in your palm and gently move them about. If they leaves are good quality then they should be dry enough to make a rustling noise in the palm.

2. Smell.

The fragrance of the tea should be pure and only of the fragrance of tea. If there is presence of charred smell or acid smell then the tea leaves are not as high quality as they should be. Good teas, particularly the fresh ones, have an aroma that is natural and fragrant like flowers rather than the stale smelling poor quality teas.

3. Taste.

This step is optional but to truly determine if you have a good quality tea then you should take some tea leaves and chew them carefully.

Taste of the leaves should be fresh and mellow, anything else could signal poorer quality.

Next step, infuse a bit of tea leaves to see if the leaves unfurl smoothly and see if they sink to the bottom slowly. This is an indication of better quality tea.

The resulting tea liquor should be emerald green or golden in colour and when you taste it the tea should be a little bitter but with long lasting sweet finish – like a wine. If the tea liquor smells bad or is dark brown then it is considered stale and of lesser quality.

4. The infused tea leaves.

The infused leaves should extend or unfurl smoothly and without impurities. Higher quality teas will be whole and without damage.

Tea Ware: Equipment and Utensils

No particular utensils are required in order to enjoy tea but at a bare minimum you need a cup, some receptacle to steep the tea and the tea itself.

If you are enjoying tea as part of a tea ceremony, more extensive utensils will be required.

Common Tea Equipment

Yixing purple clay

Purple clay is excavated from the mountains of Yixing and the area is the centre of the production of purple clay wares. Shushan region produces the fine clay for tea pots and cups and Dingshan is known for producing larger items such as basins and jars.

Purple clay is divided into zisha (purple clay), zhusha (orange red clay) and benshanluni (yellow clay). These are either used by themselves or mixed together with mineral colours to get a wide range of earth colours of brown, red and yellow. Dark green and blackish purple were developed in the 20th century.

Yixing Teapots

Yixing teapots are considered the best teapots for drinking tea in the gong fu tea ceremony. The yixing clay is said to be the best to bring out the taste, colour and aroma of the tea. These teapots are unglazed and over time will take on the flavour characteristics of the tea that it is used for. As such, tea lovers often use one teapot dedicated to one type of tea as to prevent 'contamination' of flavours.

Teacups

Chinese tea cups, and especially the ones used in the gong fu tea ceremony are low, wide and shallow. They are very small compared to Western tea cups and resemble a tiny bowl just big enough for one or two sips.

In the Gong fu tea ceremony, this is to emphasise 'quality over quantity' and makes the tea drinker concentrate and savour the taste of the tea as it's in very small amounts each time.

The shapes of the tea cups vary as well depending on the type of tea that will be drunk. The shapes of the tea cup, like wine glasses, accentuate the taste and aroma of the type of tea. You will note that Chinese tea cups do not have handles, that's why there are different shapes of tea cups too, to enables picking up a hot cup of tea without burning your fingers.

Tea Tray

A tea tray collects water during the Gong Fu tea ceremony. During the ceremony, the tea leaves are washed and it's customary to pour the water into the tea tray rather than any other receptacle. It also collects water that may be splashed around when making the tea.

Usually the tea trays have built in water reservoirs or hoses to an external one that helps transport the water away after the ceremony.

This is not necessary to drinking tea but it is part of the Gong Fu tea ceremony. You could use a substitute such as large bowl. The important part is that the first brew of the leaves is poured out in order to wash the leaves so you will need something to pour this first brew into it. The first brew is not consumed.

Tea trays are often made with elaborate design and can be made from many materials, the most common being bamboo and lacquered wood.

Gai Wan

A gai wan is a traditional porcelain covered tea cup used to make, serve and drink tea. If you only need one thing for tea drinking, make it a gai wan because it is that versatile. You can use these instead of the Yixing teapots and they do not change the taste of the tea. Their hard surface makes them flavour neutral and do not take on the flavour characteristics of the tea that it brews. Because of this, gai wans are used for evaluating and comparing teas.

Kettle

Different types of teas have different brewing and steeping times and this is controlled by the temperature of the water that is added to the tea leaves. Ensuring the correct and optimal temperature for the tea type is essential to creating the best tasting tea.

Tea lovers would use specialised kettles to select the correct temperature but for the casual tea drinker with a modern kettle, it's not necessary to have a thermometer. You simply look at the size of the bubbles to tell you whether it's at the correct temperature.

For more information regarding the correct temperature for the tea type, refer to the individual tea type.

Pitcher

The pitcher is used to stop the brewing of the tea and to serve the tea into the teacups. Brewing and steeping times vary and pouring into a pitcher will stop the brewing process just at the time that you wish. Serving from a pitcher also ensures that the tea is the same strength for each cup. Pitchers may come with lids and this is to keep the tea warm.

Chinese Tea Scoop

These are a traditional tool used to measure out tea leaves and assists in placing them inside a teapot or a gai wan. Because tea pots are small, their openings are also small making it difficult to accurately place the tea leaves inside. The Chinese tea scoop aids this as well as serving as a measure. Generally one scoop is equivalent to a Western tablespoon.

Scoops can be made from wood, metal and bone as well as other ancient and valuable materials. One should use a scoop when starting out to understand the quantities of tea leaves to use each time. Then you can adjust the dosage of tea leaves as you gain experience and develop a taste for tea.

Tongs

Tongs are used for hygienic reasons. Just like in food preparation, when making tea for others, proper food handling procedures need to be followed. Tongs are also used to pick up and clean off stray leaves from the tea tray or for transporting tea cups from the tea tray or preparation area to your guests.

Strainer

Chinese strainers have very fine meshes that are specially shaped to fit Chinese teapots and pitchers. They make sure that your tea remains clear and catches all the loose particles and impurities before drinking. It is often affixed to the pitcher before pouring the tea from the tea pot. The tea trainer is then removed from the pitcher before serving into the tea cups.

How To Store Chinese Tea

Teas should be stored in a cool dry place where temperatures do not vary much. Tea is extremely porous and absorbs odours very easily so keep away from spices or pungent things.

It's best to store tea in airtight containers rather than the plastic bags or cardboard containers that tea comes in. Tea that comes in a tin is alright as long as you can keep the lid on tight and not have it absorb outside smells.

Most teas last for about one year however there are exceptions and also depending on how you store them. For instances, if they're vacuum packed, they can last for longer than one year.

Green and white teas deteriorate much faster than fermented teas because they are oxidised by exposure to the air. If you're buying from a shop you should always ask how long the tea has been on the shelf and sitting outside before you buy. If you can, buy tea when they are re-stocked or newly in stock at your tea shop.

Vacuum packaging helps the tea last longer when stored at shops but it also has the effect of crushing the tea leaves and as a result can make the tea bitter. Transfer into an airtight container as soon as you can after purchase.

It is also recommended to store the green and white teas in the fridge inside an airtight container. This will prolong their life as they won't oxidise as fast in a fridge. It can also improve the flavour of the tea overtime but do not take it out of the fridge and store it on the shelf as the tea flavour can deteriorate quickly. Green and white teas suitable for fridge storage include: Taiwan Oolong, Tie Guan Yin and Phoenix teas.

Pu-Erh Tea mellows quickly and the flavour develops dramatically when kept in an unglazed clay jar. Keep in a cool dry place with little temperature fluctuation.

Like wine, you can 'age' tea. You can buy younger tea and store it for many years in a clay jar until you're ready to drink it. When you're ready to use the tea, break the tea into small pieces and return it to a clay jar. This will 'awaken' the tea and the flavour will start to develop more rapidly. If you don't have a clay jar a cardboard box or paper bag can be used as substitutes but beware of odours.

Some teas, such as Da Hong Pao tea should be kept in glazed porcelain jars in a cool, dry place as they improve with age. The smoky flavours develop intensely when kept in such conditions.

CHAPTER 4: TEA APPRECIATION AND TEA CEREMONY

The Tea Ceremony

- Tea pot - ideally a Yixing clay one but porcelain also works
- Tea strainer
- Kettle (stove top or electric)
- Tea pitcher
- Tea tray
- Deep plate or bowl - large enough for washing the teapot and cups and discarding used tea leaves
- Tea towel
- Water
- Loose leaf tea
- Tea pick - to unclog and clean the teapot
- Tea leaf scoop
- Tongs
- Scent cups - narrow snifter cups for appreciating the tea's aroma
- Tea cups - cups for drinking tea
- Optional: Tea snacks like dried plums and pistachios

Step One – Warming the Teapot, Sterilizing the Teacups and the Strainer

Warming up the teapot produces the best results for the tea because it reduces the temperature shift between inside the teapot and outside the teapot. Warming up the teapot first will have less of an impact on the flavour than if you didn't.

So start with filling the teapot with boiling water and let it sit. Then move onto the sterilizing the strainer and fill the teacups to sterilize and warm them. All tea cups, including the narrow scent cups should be sterilized by hot water. A good tea tray will collect the water being poured over the tea wares.

You could also sterilize the cups in the large deep bowl or plate, using the tongs to turn the cups in the water and to transport them to the tea tray again without burning your fingers.

Place your equipment where it is most handy to you and always return the equipment to the same spot so that they are there when you need them. This helps with the meditative nature of the tea ceremony too. Everything has a place and a home.

There's no need to sterilize the tea scoop, but do warm up the pitcher as well. Do the same for the pitcher as the tea pot. Pour some hot water into it and let it sit.

Once you have finished rinsing the tea cups, pour out the water from the teapot and the pitcher.

You are now ready to begin making the tea.

Step Two - Rinse The Tea Leaves

Put the kettle on again if or if you had your water keeping warm during the first step then you may use that water if it's at the right temperature.

Take the tea scoop and measure out an amount of tea according to the guidelines (under the different types of tea chapter or you can ask the person who sold you the tea or measure according to your tastes if you're experienced).

Place the tea leaves into the warm and empty teapot. Make sure the water is at the correct temperature for your type of tea. Pour the water into the teapot and allow the water to overflow until bubbles disappear and the water runs clear.

Put the lid on and immediately pour the water out. Keep the slid slight open so that when you tilt it to allow heat to escape, your tea leaves will not 'cook' but instead retain its aroma.

Step Three - First Brew

Once you've emptied the teapot again, your tea leaves have been successfully washed and are ready for the first brew.

Fill the teapot again with water and again ensuring it overflows over the top. Replace the lid and slowly count 5 seconds while you pour a little hot water over the teapot. This ensures that the temperature inside the teapot is even whilst the tea brews.

At the end of your count, pour the tea over the strainer and into the pitcher. Remember to tilt the lid of the teapot so the tea leaves don't 'cook'.

Take the tea cups with the tongs and empty them of the warming sterilising water. First pour a small amount into the snifter cups and then serve the tea in the tea cups.

Take the snifter cups and bring it up to your nose. Smell the tea for its aromas and fragrance.

Then quickly drink the tea.

The rest of the tea cups are to be enjoyed either with or without tea snacks. Savour the flavours.

Step Four - Additional Brews

Tea leaves can be brewed as many times as your tastes like. Simply repeat step three until you have finished brewing the tea. You can also experiment with different brewing times with different teas but if you're starting out, you should follow the guidelines of the type of tea that you're drinking.

If you'd like a more intense flavour and perhaps more bitter then steep or brew longer.

Gradually as you make additional brews, the flavours will become less intense and you'll know when it's time to stop brewing those tea leaves.

Step Five - Finishing Up

When you have finished brewing the tea, you remove the leaves and rinse the teapot and lid with hot water. Then place it in a cool dry place to air off. Tea is best made with a dry pot and this allows the tea oils to be absorbed into the clay. Simply rinse the rest of the tools and tea wares and leave to dry.

If you have tea remaining after you have finished and they can still be brewed for a few additional times, it's alright to leave them in the teapot with the tea closed for up to 12 hours. Do not leave any longer than that as the tea might develop mould and once that gets into the clay it will ruin the teapot. When you're ready to make more tea just add hot water.

How do I achieve the right temperature?

The most accurate way is to use a thermometer to measure the temperature of the water in the kettle. One approach is to heat the water to boiling and then let it cool down a bit before pouring into your teapot.

To cool down the water quickly you could use the following methods:

Pour water from the kettle into a glass cup and let sit 2 - 3 minutes to reach 160°F - 170°F or 5 minutes to reach 140°F - 150°F. Then pour into your teapot and brew for the desired length of time. You may need to adjust the sitting time based on the size of your glass cup and the amount of water.

Pour water from the kettle into a cool glass or ceramic cup and pour back and forth between cups until the desired temperature is reached. Then pour into your teapot and brew.

Traditional Chinese method of identifying the right water temperature

There are essentially five identifiable stages in the boiling of water:

Shrimp Eyes: The first, tiny bubbles that appear. Around 70°C/158°F - 80°C/176°F

Crab Eyes: Slightly larger bubbles. 80°C/176°F - 85°C/185°F

Fish Eyes: Good size bubbles will form; this is the temperature where delicate green, white and some of the yellow teas will brew well. 85°C/185°F - 90°C/194°F

String of Pearls: Bubbles are beginning to break the surface and cling to the sides of the pan. Everyday green teas, many higher grade teas and some black teas do very well at this temperature. 90°C/194°F - 95°C/203°F

Dragon Eyes: This is a rolling boil. Large bubbles are breaking the surface.

Very few green teas will yield positive results at this temperature, but black teas, Oolongs and Pu-erhs can be steeped with this water. One note, if you choose to brew at this temperature, you will bring the taste of the tea out quickly. The leaves will release much of their flavor early in the steep and as a result provide a full taste while probably knocking off or blunting some of its more subtle notes. 95°C/203°F - 100°C/212°F

Old man water: is over boiled or 'flat' water 100°C/212°F

General Brewing Times

Here are some general guidelines:

- Japanese Green Teas: 1-2 minutes
- Chinese Green Teas: 2-3 minutes
- White Teas: 2-5 minutes
- Green Oolong Teas: 2-3 minutes
- Dark Oolong Teas: 3-5 minutes
- Black Teas: 3-5 minutes
- Herbal Infusions: 5-10 minutes

Tea Snacks

As it is with most beverages, tea can also be paired with food. In fact, in tea's long history, it has always accompanied food and as we have seen throughout its history in China, tea is now the main beverage of choice at meal times.

But since tea is also enjoyed in between meals, naturally, snacks have emerged as accompaniments. Like beer to izakaya, biscotti with an Italian espresso, Chinese tea also has snacks that compliment it well.

With certain snacks, it can enhance the flavour of your teas, For example, sweet snacks will taste better with green and black teas, while salty snacks will help enrich the flavor of oolong tea. So experiment and experiment often to find the snacks that compliments your choice of tea.

"The 3 precious tea snacks"

"The 3 precious tea snacks" are rose crunchy candy, salty peach slice and sticky candy.

Not only are these delicious snacks, they are also aesthetically appealing and will sure to impress guests when you bring them out in your tea ceremonies.

The rose crunchy candies are made by pickling fresh roses in sugar for approximately 5 months. The long processing time is to ensure that the best rose aromas are produced. Tea snacks, although only accompaniments to tea, should also be produced with pride and to a high standard.

After the pickling phase, the resulting product is worked into a bar shaped candy and served as small slices. The best rose crunchy candy has the perfect balance between chewy and crunchy and has the most remarkable rose scent. It should be light pink and anything more than that would indicate additional coloring was added.

The salty peach slices are made of rice powder, sugar, flour, oil, salt, walnut and black sesame and smell like baked peaches. This is a steamed snack that is formed into a bar shape as it cools and then cut into slices again to serve.

The sticky candy is a very traditional snack that involves the working of 4 basic ingredients: flour, sugar, peanuts and white sesame seeds. The best kind of sticky candy will be chewy forever and won't dry out or get hard as you store it. In recent years, sticky candy has been enhanced by the introduction of different flavours and additional nuts such as walnuts.

Sichuan Spicy Chicken Feet

Chicken feet may be what we cast off when we buy our chickens but in China they're quite a delicacy. You might want to skip these in your tea ceremony but as a snack, they're absolutely delicious. You just have to be willing to give it a try.

The chicken feet are soaked in sauce consisting of chilli and vinegar for several days which leaves the chicken feet crunchy and full of flavor. The strong flavour is perfect with certain types of teas but careful not to pair the chicken feet with the delicate fragrant teas as they'll overpower the flavour of the tea.

It's called Sichuan Spicy chicken feet because of the Sichuan peppers added to the marinating mix and also because it's from the Sichuan province. Additional peppers can be added or chilli oil can be added when serving if you like spicy foods.

Fried Dough Twists

The fried dough twist is also a national treasure that is often served not only with tea but also as meal staples. The fried dough twists are made of a mixture of flour, sugar and salt. The resulting dough is squeezed and twisted and then fried in hot oil. They come out crunchy and full of flavorful and perfect with oolong.

Chinese cakes and pastries

Chinese cakes and pastries are distinctly different from the Western pastries but nonetheless delicious with tea. Chinese cakes and pastries are flakier and often contain morsels of goodness in the center. For instances, a winter melon pastry named the 'wife cake' is spectacular with black tea and the almond cookies or egg rolls (not the fried ones at your local Chinese) are great with all teas.

Dried prunes, dried orange peels, preserved tangerine or mandarin peel

Preserved citrus peel is the most common tea snack that you can find and are a stable of tea ceremonies. The tastes of these are often compared to green tea because they are bitter at first and then leave the person with a sweet after taste

CHAPTER 5: DIFFERENT TYPES OF TEAS

Green Tea

Green tea is made from the new shoots of the tea plant. Green tea is an unfermented tea and undergoes a pan-firing process right after the leaves have been plucked. It is the most common type of tea in China and when infused the tea is yellowish green with a fresh aroma. It is pale in colour and has a sharp flavour.

It is produced primarily in the provinces of Jiangxi, Anhui, and Zhejiang.

Green teas are better when brewed at lower temperatures as the overall flavour can be 'sweet'.

Amino acids dissolve at 140°F (60 °C) while tannins dissolve at 176°F (80°C). Therefore, brewing green tea at lower temperatures will ensure that its sweet and complex flavors will not be overpowered by the bitter-tasting flavors.

As a general guideline, green teas taste best when brewed at temperatures between 140°F - 185°F. Steeping time should be balanced with water temperature: the lower the temperature, the longer the tea can be steeped.

Green teas do not require much brewing time as too long a steeping time will result in more bitterness and a less balanced flavor.

Experiment between 1-3 minutes for Chinese green teas.

Famous green teas include: Dragon Well Tea (Long Jing), Anji Bai Cha, Mao Jian, Pouchong (Baozhong).

Black Tea

Black tea is called Red tea in Chinese so you will often see it listed as either Chinese black tea or red tea. Both refer to black tea. Black tea is the second largest category of Chinese tea and is a fully fermented tea. It's called red tea in Chinese because of its bright reddish colour when infused and a rich and aromatic flavour.

Black tea made in China usually comprises of whole tea leaves or buds as opposed to the chopped black tea made in India and Sri Lanka. The new shoots of the tea leaves are wilted, rolled, fermented and then dried before grading and packing.

Tea steeping times vary depending on the cut of the leaf but as a general rule brew for 2 -3 minutes for fine cut leaf and up to 5 minutes for large leaf black tea. Brew the tea with water that is that is 190 °F to 200°F.

Black teas can be brewed additional times after the first brew. Brewing additional times will require less steeping time than the first brew and if brewing at higher temperatures the flavours will be released earlier and subsequent brews will not be as intense.

Famous black teas include: Lapsang Souchong, Keemun Hao Ya, Bai Lin Gong Fu, Dian Hong (Yunnan Black), Fu Shou Mei (Sugarcane Black), Yunnan Gold Pearls

Oolong Tea

Oolong tea is a partially fermented tea. It is partially oxidised and this is controlled by the pan-firing process. Once infused the tea is a bright yellow and has a fresh rich flavour with a long-lasting aftertaste. Fujian, Guangdong and Taiwan are the main areas that this tea is produced. As such oolong is particularly popular for people of these regions and was the ones that gave rise to the gong fu ceremony.

The name *oolong tea* came into the English language from the Chinese name meaning "black dragon tea". In Chinese, oolong teas are also known as *qingcha* or "dark green teas".

To brew oolong, use water with temperatures at 180°F – 200°F or by the Chinese classification: 'string of pearl' water. Oolong teas are generally steeped for 30 seconds to a minute, and can be brewed for another 6 to 8 times, depending on the type of oolong.

Famous oolong teas include: Iron Buddha (Tie Guan Yin), Big Red Robe (Da

Hong Pao), Dan Cong Tea, Ali Shan.

White Tea

White tea is a slightly fermented tea and is mainly produced in Fujian province.

It is characterised by the high content of succulent, whitish, and hairy leaf-buds with a slight greenish tinge. This physical appearance gives the tea its name. The tea leaves are minimally processed and are a product unique to China. As a result of little processing, the infusion is a bright yellowish green and has a mild to mellow flavour.

The ideal water temperature for brewing white tea is between 170 – 185 degrees F (76 to 85 degrees) and should be brewed for around 1- 2 minutes. As white tea is a very lightly fermented tea, the tea leaves require a longer brewing time than most teas and can be steeped up to five minutes.

White tea can be brewed an additional 5-6 times.

Some famous white teas include: Silver Needle (Yin Zhen) and White Peony (Bai Mu Dan)

Yellow Tea

Yellow tea is a slightly fermented tea. Yellow tea is made in a similar fashion as green tea but with an added step of being steamed or a 'smothering' process. The tea leaves are placed under a damp cloth after oxidation that gives the leaves a unique yellow colouring and slightly sweeter taste.

To brew yellow tea use water around 160°F - 170°F. Brew for up to 2 minutes and the tea can be brewed again for another 2-3 times.

Famous yellow teas include: Meng Ding Hu Yellow Tea, Golden Dragon Yellow Tea

Pu-erh Tea

Pu-erh tea is a post-fermented tea that can be made from green, oolong or black tea. The heaping procedure helps to generate its unique colour, aroma, and flavour. The best known variety is from Pu-erh from Yunnan Province. All types of pu-erh can be stored to mature before consumption, which is why it is commonly labelled with year and region of production.

The tea infusion has a brownish red colour and its flavour is rich and mellow.

Pu-erh is also known as 'hei cha' or black tea in Chinese but not to be confused with the black tea types that are known as red teas in Chinese. The spelling of pu-erh also varies between Pu-erh Tea, Pu'erh Tea, Pu erh, Bolay Tea.

To brew pu-erh you should use water that is boiling or 200°F – 210°F and steep for 10-20 seconds. Because of the short steep times and high temperature of the water, pu-erh tea can be brewed up to an additional 10 times and adding 5-10 seconds of steeping time for each new brew.

Scented Tea

Also known as smoked tea or fragrant tea, this is a variety unique to China. It is a blend of tea base and fragrant flowers processed in a specific way so that the tea leaves can absorb the floral fragrance of fresh flowers. The strands are tight and even, with a distinct floral scent. Colour of tea is light amber and leaves are fine and tender, even and bright. Most scented tea won't be sold with the flowers themselves, the tea has already absorbed the aroma during the slow processing.

Common varieties are jasmine oolong tea and rose red tea. Although it's a common variety, jasmine flowers are not originally from China. It was imported from central Asia during the Tang Dynasty and nowadays Sichuan Province has grown to be one of the largest centers of jasmine tea production in China, alongside Fujian Province.

To brew scented tea, use water temperature around 190F. For pearl shaped tea, you need to infuse about 2-3 minutes for the first infusion to give it time to open and bring out the flavor. For loose scented tea, brew your first infusion for about 1-2 minutes. Scented teas can be brewed for an additional

4-5 times.

Blooming Tea

Also known as artistic scented tea and artistic tea, it features different kinds of flowers blooming in the brewed tea to form unique, elegant, colourful, and attractive patterns. While enjoying the sweet taste of tea, you can also admire painting-like compositions in the cup. It is a pleasurable experience of grace, fragrance, and amusement. Blooming tea is also a health tonic. Major varieties are Jasmine Fairy and Wild Green Peony. In order to take advantage of the artistic unfurling of the blooming tea, a glass teapot is recommended.

To brew blooming tea, the first steep is to let the blooming flower 'bloom' properly. As blooming teas are tightly bundled, it is essential to use water just below boiling point for them to properly bloom. It only takes a minute or 2 for a flowering tea to bloom and another 1 minute to fully unfurl. As soon as it reaches full bloom, it is ready to be poured over gently for your first cup of tea. The first steep will have a strong flavor with an intense aroma of the flowers that are used.

The blooming tea can be brewed for an additional 2-3 times.

Tea Bricks

Tea bricks are tea leaves piled, steamed, and compressed into bricks or other shapes. Raw ingredients are raw dark green tea, dark green tea, processed pack tea, and other processed crude tea leaves. Tea bricks are usually made with red or black tea, and most varieties are coarse. Colour of dry tea is brown black. Colour of tea is clear yellow or clear red. Common varieties are Toucha, bamboo tea, Fuzhuan brick tea, green brick tea, and Kang brick tea.

Cha Gao

Cha gao is now more known as instant pu-erh tea. 'Cha Gao' literally means 'tea paste'. This specialty of Yunnan province uses a technique to extract the liquid from the tea leaves and then solidifies the liquid into shapes which can easily be dissolved in water to make tea. Unfortunately, imperial techniques employed during the Qing dynasty were lost with the collapse of the Qing dynasty in 1911, and attempts to revive the industry in subsequent decades fell short and the practice of making tea-paste practically vanished. Now, with modern technology it is possible to produce tea-paste that is of similar quality to that which was produced during the Qing dynasty.

Cha gao concentrates the chemicals found in Pu-erh tea to a very condensed and potent form and during the Qing dynasty, it was used as a form of medicine.

To brew cha goa you do not need much because it's a concentrated pu-erh tea. Use one unit and pour boiling water into a teapot and let the cha gao dissolves completely before serving. You can either place the cha gao in the teapot first and then pour over the water or you could simply add the cha gao into the water in the teapot.

CHAPTER 6: DIFFERENT REGIONS OF CHINESE TEAS

Fujian Province

Fujian Province is located on the South East coast of China, facing Taiwan. The province has been developing its local tea-growing techniques since the Song dynasty. In the nineteenth century, Fujian was the undisputed leader in the production of tea in China, and hence, the entire globe.

The province is famous for the quality of its teas, in particular its Oolong and White varieties, however, it is also home to some renowned Back teas such as Lapsang Souchong and Keemen Black. Undoubtedly, Fujian is the finest tea growing province in the country.

Hubei Province

China's Hubei Province, home to China's first and foremost tea specialist, Lu Yu. Tea Production in Hubei started all the way back in the eighth century. Its eastern counties, bordering the province of Anhui, are considered some of the oldest tea-growing areas in the country.

Most of the tea plantations are located on mountain slopes at an altitude of 1,000 meters above sea level. The province grows and produces Green and Yellow teas.

Hunan Province

This central province is one of the main centers of tea production in China. In the 19th and early 20th century, Hunan produced almost half the total volume of Chinese tea. Tea growing is encouraged by favorable soil and a warm, temperate climate.

Henan Province

Henan Province is located in the central part of the country and is bordered to the south by the provinces of Hubei and Anhui. Its main tea-growing areas are located in the south, which have the same natural conditions as the two above mentioned neighboring provinces. However, tea does not play such an important role in the economic life of Henan province, as it does, for example, in Hubei province. Nevertheless, Henan Green tea is of excellent quality.

Zhejiang Province

Other than a few small areas bordering Shanghai, the whole of Zhejiang province is one huge plantation. Red soil and a mild subtropical climate contribute to the development of a tea growing region that produces Green tea all year round. It is here that you will find the world-famous *Dragonwell* green tea. Zhejiang today accounts for almost three quarters of total tea production in China.

Anhui Province

Located in the lower reaches of the Yangtze River, Anhui is a major tea-growing province in China. The province is divided into two regions - the north and the south, with tea growing in the northern region dating back to the Tang dynasty (618AD-907AD).

Guangdong Province

Guangdong province stretches along the coast of the South China Sea and has tropical climate and an average temperature that exceeds 20 degrees all year round, allowing tea collection to be carried out 10 months of the year. In Guangdong, just like in Yunnan, there is also an abundance of wild, uncultivated tea bushes. The province is not a major supplier of tea, but has huge potential.

Guangxi Province

In this southern province, bordering Vietnam, tea culture has only begun to gain ground in recent years. The main plantations are located in the east of the province, near the city of Guilin.

Guizhou Province

Guizhou is bordered by Sichuan to the west and Yunnan to the south. Despite being surrounded by so many famous tea-growing provinces, tea culture has not seen any significant development here. Tea is none the less cultivated throughout the province on numerous small plantations.

Sichuan Province

This south-western province was the first part of China to see the popularization of tea culture, consumed en masse as an everyday drink rather than a form of medicine. Today, anyone passing through Sichuan will not fail to notice the central role it still plays in people's lives. A temperate, humid climate allows a lot of tea to be produced in this region and it remains today one of China's major tea producing provinces, producing many well known brands of Green and Black teas.

Yunnan Province

Yunnan Province is located in southwest China. Tea Culture in Yunnan dates back to ancient times and is regarded by Chinese scientists as the home of tea and indeed, it is here that you will find the oldest wild tea trees in China. 98% of tea produced in Yunnan today is of the *Pu-erh* variety.

Jiangsu Province

Bordering Zhejiang, Jiangsu Province has been growing tea since the seventh century. Washed by the waters of the Yellow Sea, the province has good natural conditions for tea which is grown together with fruit, producing the deliciously fruity *Spring Snail* Green tea.

Printed in Great Britain
by Amazon